COMMUNITY · CONNECTIONS ?

HOW DO WE LIVE TOGETHER?
SNAKES

BY LUCIA RAATMA

Published in the United States of America by Cherry Lake Publishing
Ann Arbor, Michigan
www.cherrylakepublishing.com

Content Adviser: Stephen S. Ditchkoff, PhD, Associate Professor, School of Forestry and
Wildlife Sciences, Auburn University
Reading Adviser: Cecilia Minden-Cupp, PhD, Literacy Consultant

Photo Credits: Cover and page 1, ©Ben Laney, used under license from Shutterstock, Inc.;
page 5, ©Stevebyland/Dreamstime.com; page 7, ©Leighton Photography & Imaging, used under
license from Shutterstock, Inc.; page 9, ©danmiami, used under license from Shutterstock, Inc.;
page 11, ©iStockphoto.com/Snowleopard1; page 13, ©Ryan M. Bolton, used under license from
Shutterstock, Inc.; page 15, ©Rdodson/Dreamstime.com; page 17, ©iStockphoto.com/sbrogan;
page 19, ©iStockphoto.com/c-photo; page 21, ©iStockphoto.com/shannonforehand

LIBRARY OF CONGRESS CATALOGING-IN-PUBLICATION DATA
Raatma, Lucia.
  How do we live together? Snakes / by Lucia Raatma.
    p. cm.—(Community connections)
  Includes bibliographical references and index.
  ISBN-13: 978-1-60279-620-1
  ISBN-10: 1-60279-620-3
  1. Snakes—Juvenile literature. 2. Human-animal relationships—Juvenile
literature. 3. Urban animals—Juvenile literature. I. Title.
  QL666.O6R235 2010
  597.96—dc22   2009027886

Cherry Lake Publishing would like to acknowledge the
work of The Partnership for 21st Century Skills. Please
visit www.21stcenturyskills.org for more information.

Printed in the United States of America
Corporate Graphics Inc.
January 2010
CLSP06

SNAKES

CONTENTS

HOW DO WE LIVE TOGETHER?

WHAT'S THAT IN THE GRASS?

You're playing in the backyard. You see something move. Your dog starts to bark. What's that in the grass? It **slithers** away. That is when you realize it's a snake!

4

Have you ever spotted a snake in your yard?

Snakes are common in yards, wooded areas, and other outdoor spaces. They are usually looking for food. They also sleep among leaves and in hollow logs. Many snakes are harmless. Others can be very dangerous.

Garter snakes are common in North America.

Many people are afraid of snakes. They often think they should kill any snakes they see. But snakes play an important part in the **ecosystem**. They help keep nature in balance. Let's take some time to learn more about snakes.

Some snakes climb trees. Others swim through water, depending on where they live.

LOOK!

Have you ever taken a good look at a snake's skin? Snakes shed their skin each year. They often do this several times. You might be surprised that snakes are not slimy. Their skin is smooth and dry.

9

A CLOSER LOOK AT SNAKES

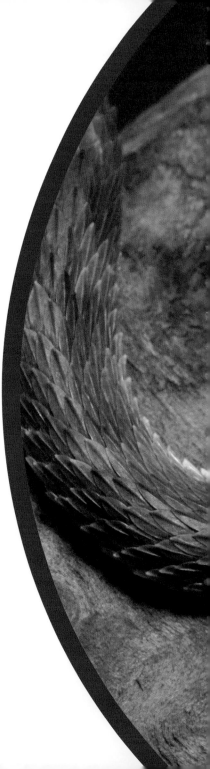

Snakes are **reptiles**. They live on every **continent** except Antarctica. There are almost 3,000 kinds of snakes around the world. Some snakes are huge. Pythons and anacondas can be 33 feet (10 meters) long. Other snakes are very small.

Snakes come in many colors and sizes. Bush vipers, such as this one, live in Africa.

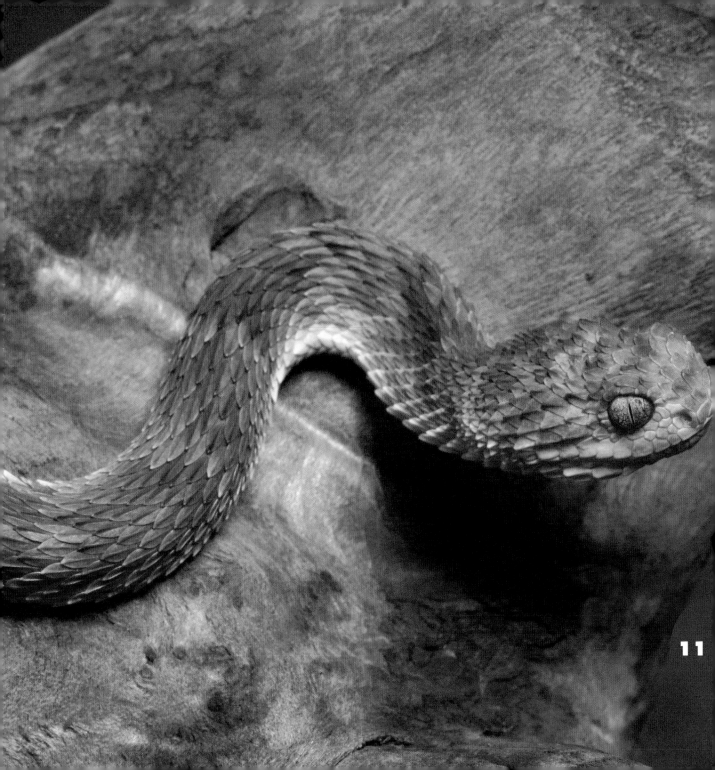

Harmless snakes include garter snakes and rat snakes. Rattlesnakes, coral snakes, and copperheads are a different story. These snakes use their **venom** to kill animals. They eat mice and birds. They also eat frogs and other animals. Some snakes are **constrictors**. They squeeze and kill their **prey** before eating it.

Rattlesnakes rattle their tails to scare away other animals.

THINK!

How are snakes helpful? One way is through what they eat. Many snakes eat mice and insects. This helps control the population of these animals. Can you think of reasons why that is a good thing?

Snakes are cold-blooded. Their body temperature changes with the temperature of their surroundings. That's why snakes are seen more often when it is warm. They enjoy lying in the sun on a summer day.

It is smart to learn about the habits of snakes. That way, we can find ways to safely share the outdoors with them.

This kingsnake warms itself in the sun in Arizona.

SHARING OUTDOOR SPACES

Some snakes are dangerous. Some are not. Always keep your distance to be safe. Tell an adult if you see a snake in your yard. Don't try to touch it. Most snakes do not want to harm people. They usually bite only when they think they are in danger.

People and their pets can be very scary to a snake. Always be careful if you see one.

How can you and your family stay safe? You can take simple steps.

Keep your yard neat. Make sure the grass is kept short. Clean up piles of leaves or other materials. Snakes might want to hide there. Wear sturdy boots when hiking. They protect your feet from snakebites better than sneakers or sandals. Always watch where you step.

Some places have signs to warn visitors about snakes living there.

Do you like to play outside? Look carefully before reaching under bushes to grab something. A startled snake will bite!

Remember, it is important to respect snakes and their space. That way, we can all share the great outdoors!

The outdoors is a great place to be. Just remember that other animals live there, too!

Is your family thinking about owning a pet snake? Talk to an expert from a zoo or wildlife department. Ask questions. Is caring for snakes expensive? Do they need a lot of attention? What are some other important questions to ask?

GLOSSARY

constrictors (kuhn-STRIK-turz) snakes that squeeze and kill their prey before eating it

continent (KON-tuh-nuhnt) one of seven large landmasses on Earth

ecosystem (EE-koh-siss-tuhm) a community of animals and plants interacting with one another and with their surroundings

prey (PRAY) animals that are hunted and eaten by other animals

reptiles (REP-tilez) cold-blooded animals that have backbones, usually lay eggs, and are covered in scales or hard plates

shed (SHED) let a natural covering fall or drop off

slithers (SLITH-urz) moves by sliding and twisting along a surface

venom (VEN-uhm) poison produced by certain animals, such as some kinds of snakes

FIND OUT MORE

BOOKS

Bredeson, Carmen. *Fun Facts about Snakes!* Berkeley Heights, NJ: Enslow Elementary, 2008.

Mattern, Joanne. *Copperheads.* Mankato, MN: Capstone Press, 2009.

WEB SITES

PAWSKids.org: Garter Snakes
www.pawskids.org/wildlife/washington_wildlife/garter_snakes.html
Learn more about one common type of snake.

San Diego Zoo Kid Territory—Crafts: Snake Mobile
www.sandiegozoo.org/kids/craft_snake_mobile.html
Get creative with this snake art project.

INDEX

24

ABOUT THE AUTHOR

Lucia Raatma has written dozens of books for young readers. She and her family live in the Tampa Bay area of Florida. They once had a black racer snake sneak into their house through a gap in the sliding glass door!